Daddy Can I Go Fishing?
The Adventures of Billy Fix

Billy Fix

DEDICATION

I dedicate my book, *Daddy Can I Go Fishing*, to my parents, the late Tony and Vadna Fix, my wife, Dottie, my Children Leona & Toby and Lynnette & Jason, plus my four grandchildren Lydia, Joel, Lucy and Jerod. I thank Jesus Christ my Savior, for gracing me with a great family. I dedicate this and all my work to Him.

CONTENTS

ACKNOWLEDGMENTS

I want to acknowledge all the children in the churches I have been blessed to pastor, for teaching me how to relate to a younger crowd. I have not forgotten all the conversations I have had with the innocent and honest children. I have learned much from them. I want to acknowledge Dottie Miller, former Director of Children's Ministries for the Free Methodist Church of North America, and my good friend Rick Jewett, former Child Evangelist for investing in me. I also want to acknowledge my many teachers at the Fellowship of Christian Magicians for teaching me the various arts that are effective in teaching children; magic, ventriloquism, puppetry, art, comedy, music, paper tears, and object lessons with a message. .

Hello! My name is Billy. When I was four years old,

Daddy told me I was too little to go fishing.

Now I'm five. So, I asked Mommy,

"Will Daddy take me fishing? I am bigger now.

Do you think Daddy will say I am too little?"

Mom was busy washing dishes.

She stooped down to look into my eyes.

"Billy, you are growing bigger every day,

but it is up to your Daddy."

I asked my brother, "Will Daddy take me fishing?"

Jimmy messed up my hair and said, "You are too little."

My baby sister, Joan, was eating a cookie.

I asked her if she thought I was too little to go fishing.

She just ate her cookie. She could not talk yet.

I was happy that she was little and I was big."

1

Boxer, my little puppy, wagged his tiny tail,

and he licked my fingers as I petted his face.

I felt good because Boxer was little, and I was big --

maybe big enough to go fishing!

Daddy had come home from work, he looked at me and said, "Hi, Billy, how is my big boy?" I said, "Great, Daddy." I was very happy - He called me a big boy! – Maybe big enough to go fishing.

That night, when I went to bed, Mommy and Daddy tucked me in. Dad told me I would have my own fishing pole. "Really?" I asked. Dad said, "yes,"and then told me to get some sleep."

When I woke up the next day I ran to ask Mommy,

"Is it Saturday?" She stooped down and said,

"Not yet, Billy, but soon." Mommy told me that on

Saturday she would pack a lunch for me and

Daddy with some snacks I would like.

One day I woke up and Mommy told me that tomorrow was the day, Daddy and I were going fishing, and later that night, we were going to catch worms.

That night, Daddy took a flashlight in one hand and we went out into the yard. He shined the flashlight on the ground. We saw a long worm. He told me to grab it but I was afraid. Daddy grabbed it and put it in a can.

One, two, three, four, five, six, seven, eight, nine, ten. We caught ten worms! Dad put a worm in my hand and then I was not afraid anymore. I put the worm back in the can. Dad set the can of worms beside our fishing poles.

Daddy woke me up early. He drank coffee and I ate cereal. I was ready to go fishing. Mommy packed our lunch and snacks. Daddy put everything in the trunk of the car. We got in the car and Daddy started driving to the river.

On the way to the river, Daddy took me to the bait shop. When I looked into the big tub, I saw a million tiny fish. Daddy called them minnows. The man put water in our bucket and gave us some minnows. I tried to count them but they were swimming too fast. Watching them was fun.

I got back in the car and Daddy drove down a bumpy road. All of a sudden, the road ended. There was a big sign that Daddy read. "Stop, Road Ends, Stop!" And, stop we did. Was the fishing trip over? Daddy parked the car and opened the trunk. He took out the poles, the chairs, the worms, the minnows, the tackle box and our lunch.

29

I carried my chair, the worms and my pole, and Daddy carried the rest. Our arms were full. I followed Daddy onto a path high above the river. I loved this path because I could see the river. We were careful watching out for rocks, weeds, branches and briars. At times it was scary but we made it to the river.

Daddy told me to wait until I felt a tug on the pole.

He told me, "When you feel the tug, pull up on

your pole and bring the fish in."

I waited a long time.

Then, I felt a tug on my pole, then another,

and another. I lifted my pole. No fish.

I put the fishing line back in the water. I waited again.

Soon, I felt another tug on my pole, so I lifted it up.

I caught my first fish! "Good job!" said Dad.

We fished all day.

We caught fish, ate lunch, talked much and told jokes. I loved fishing with Daddy, and we had so much fun.

When the sun was low in the sky, it was time to

go home. On the way home, I asked Daddy,

"Can we go fishing again?" Daddy said,

"Real soon."

The People Pastor Billy Fix and Grandpa

ABOUT THE AUTHOR

Author, Billy Fix, has a Doctorate in Theology. He enjoyed reading and encouraging his children to read. Pastor Bill Fix is known as the People Pastor and he: * Is a grandfather (Papa) of four wonderful grandchildren. He read them stories and encouraged them to be good readers as he listened to them read.   * Understands that early reading is vitally important to success in school and later in an occupation.   * Is a children's entertainer and knows how to relate to children.   * He was a successful children's pastor before becoming a Lead Pastor. The full color illustrations will help the child remember the story and tell it back, after it is read to them. Although this is fiction, it is based upon the Author's early fishing adventures with his dad. Daddy Can I Go Fishing, is a book that is realistic. A young boy's dream of going fishing is realistic and the dream grows as the fishing day approaches. Hope is birthed and finally experienced by little five year old Billy. The colorful animations make the story come alive and can encourage a natural conversation between parent and child. Daddy Can I Go Fishing is: * A Book your child will enjoy having read to them   * A book your child will enjoy telling back to you   * A book your child will eventually love to read When you sit down with your child to read this book It should be an enjoyable event. A child's humor is different than adult humor. Children laugh at word pictures. In the book Billy's older brother messes up Billy's hair and his baby sister eats cookies but can't talk. Boxer, is a dog that chases a thrown ball and fishing with Dad was a good experience. Enjoy reading, Daddy Can I Go Fishing?

Made in the USA
Monee, IL
31 August 2020